Service Center Performance.

APRIL 2123

Authored by: Charles P. Hillier

Improving Service Center Performance

Maximizing performance

Service center performance refers to the level of efficiency and effectiveness with which a service center operates in meeting the needs and expectations of its customers. It involves measuring the quality of the service provided, the timeliness of the service, the level of customer satisfaction, and the cost-effectiveness of the service center's operations. Performance metrics may include response time, customer satisfaction ratings, Fixed first visit rate, and other indicators of service quality and efficiency. Ultimately, the goal of service center performance is to ensure that customers receive high-quality, timely, and cost-effective service that meets or exceeds their Expatiations.

". Continuous improvement is essential for service center performance, and it involves planning, implementing, monitoring, reviewing, and adjusting improvement initiatives based on data and metrics, involving employees at all levels"

Introduction to Service Center Performance

Definition of vehicle service center performance
Vehicle service center performance refers to the effectiveness and efficiency of a facility that provides maintenance, repair, and other services for automobiles, trucks, or other vehicles. It involves various aspects such as the quality of work performed, customer satisfaction, turnaround time, productivity, profitability, and adherence to industry standards and regulations. Key performance indicators (KPIs) that may be used to measure vehicle service center performance include customer retention rate, first-time fix rate, average repair time, revenue per repair order, technician productivity, and overall profitability. Ultimately, a high performing vehicle service center should be able to provide reliable and timely services that meet the needs of its customers while ensuring profitability and compliance with applicable regulations.

Importance of vehicle service center performance for customer satisfaction and business success

Vehicle service center performance is critical for both customer satisfaction and business success. Here are some reasons why:

1. Customer satisfaction: A well-performing service center ensures that customers receive high-quality services that meet their expectations. This can lead to higher levels of customer satisfaction, which can translate into repeat business, positive word-of-mouth recommendations, and an enhanced reputation for the service center.
2. Competitive advantage: In a competitive market, a service center that performs well is more likely to attract

and retain customers than one that does not. This can give the service center a competitive advantage and help it to stand out from the competition.

3. Increased profitability: A service center that performs well is likely to be more profitable than one that does not. This is because it can complete repairs more quickly and efficiently, reduce the number of reworks, and minimize wastage of resources, resulting in lower costs and higher revenues.
4. Compliance with regulations: Compliance with industry regulations is critical for any
5. service center. A well-performing service center ensures that it adheres to all relevant
6. regulations, which can help it to avoid penalties, fines, and other legal consequences that can negatively impact the business.
7. Employee satisfaction: A well-performing service center can lead to greater employee satisfaction, which can result in reduced employee turnover and improved productivity.

This can lead to increased profits, as well as a better work environment for employees.

In summary, the importance of vehicle service center performance for customer satisfaction and business success cannot be overstated. It is critical for ensuring customer satisfaction, attracting and retaining customers, achieving profitability, complying with regulations, and fostering employee satisfaction.

Overview of key metrics for measuring Vehicle service center performance

Several key metrics can be used to measure the performance of a vehicle
service center. These metrics can provide insights into various aspects of the service center's operations, including customer satisfaction, productivity, and profitability. Here are some of the most common metrics used to measure vehicle service center performance:

1. Customer retention rate: This metric measures the percentage of customers who return to the service center for additional services. A high retention rate indicates that customers are satisfied with the service center's work and are likely to return for future repairs or maintenance.
2. First-time fix rate: This metric measures the percentage of repairs that are completed correctly on the first visit. A high first-time fix rate indicates that the service center is efficient and effective in diagnosing and repairing vehicles, reducing the need for repeat visits.
3. Average repair time: This metric measures the amount of time it takes to complete a repair. A low average repair time indicates that the service center is efficient and can
4. complete repairs quickly, reducing customer wait times and increasing productivity.
5. Revenue per repair order: This metric measures the amount of revenue generated per repair order. A high revenue per repair order indicates that the service center is generating more revenue per customer, which can increase profitability.

6. Technician productivity: This metric measures the number of repairs completed by a technician over a specific time period. A high technician productivity rate indicates that the service center is efficient and effective in managing its workforce.
7. Overall profitability: This metric measures the service center's profitability, taking into account revenue, expenses, and other factors. A high profitability rate indicates that the service center is generating more revenue than it is spending, resulting in a net profit.

These metrics can provide valuable insights into the performance of a vehicle service center and help identify areas for improvement. By monitoring these metrics over time, service center managers can track progress and make data-driven decisions to optimize their operations and improve their business results.

Understanding customer needs and expectations

Understanding customer needs and expectations is critical to the success of any vehicle
service center. By understanding what customers want and expect, a service center can
tailor its services to meet those needs and provide a superior customer experience. Here are some key factors to consider when understanding customer needs and expectations:

1. Communication: Customers expect clear and transparent communication from the service center throughout the repair process. This includes regular updates on the status of their vehicle, explanations of

the work being performed, and any additional recommendations or costs.

2. Quality of work: Customers expect high-quality workmanship and attention to detail from the service center. This includes using quality parts and equipment, following industry standards and best practices, and performing repairs accurately and efficiently.

3. Convenience: Customers value convenience and expect the service center to provide flexible scheduling options, timely repairs, and a comfortable waiting area. Some customers may also appreciate amenities such as Wi-Fi, refreshments, or loaner vehicles.

4. Price: Customers expect fair and transparent pricing from the service center, with no hidden fees or charges. They also value competitive pricing and may shop around for the best value.

5. Customer service: Customers expect friendly and knowledgeable customer service from the service center staff. This includes being greeted promptly, having their questions answered clearly, and receiving personalized recommendations and advice.

By understanding these factors and engaging with customers to gather feedback and
insights, a service center can improve its ability to meet customer needs and expectations. This can lead to increased customer satisfaction, repeat business, and a positive reputation in the community

Strategies for developing exceptional customer service.

Developing exceptional customer service is essential for any vehicle service center looking to stand out from the competition and build a loyal customer base. Here are some strategies that can help service centers develop exceptional customer service:

1. Train employees: Providing comprehensive and ongoing training to employees is critical for ensuring that they have the knowledge, skills, and attitudes needed to provide exceptional customer service. This includes training in communication, technical skills, and customer service best practices.
2. Foster a customer-centric culture: Service centers should create a culture that prioritizes the customer experience, with an emphasis on empathy, respect, and attention to detail. This culture should be embodied by all employees, from the front desk to the technicians.
3. Provide personalized service: Offering personalized service that meets the unique needs of each customer can help service centers build lasting relationships with their customers. This may include offering tailored recommendations, remembering customer preferences, and providing follow-up communication after service appointments.
4. Use technology to enhance the customer experience: Technology can be used to enhance the customer experience in a variety of ways, such as providing online scheduling options, sending appointment reminders, and offering digital communication

channels.

5. Gather customer feedback: Collecting and analyzing
    customer feedback is critical for identifying areas for
    improvement and ensuring that the service center is
    meeting customer needs and expectations. This
    feedback can be collected through surveys, reviews,
    or direct communication with customers.
6. Resolve issues promptly: When issues do arise, service
    centers should work to resolve them promptly and
    effectively. This includes listening to the customer,
    taking responsibility for the issue, and offering a
    solution that meets the customer's needs.

By implementing these strategies, service centers can develop
exceptional customer service that sets them apart from the
competition and builds a loyal customer base.

Developing effective communications skills

Effective communication skills are essential for anyone working
in a vehicle service center, as they help build trust with
customers and ensure that work is completed accurately and
efficiently. Here are some strategies that can help develop
effective communication skills:

1. Listen actively: Effective communication starts with active
    listening. This means paying attention to what the
    customer is saying, asking clarifying questions, and
    acknowledging their concerns or questions.
2. Speak clearly and concisely: Communication should be
    clear and concise, avoiding technical jargon and using
    language that the customer can understand.

3. Provide regular updates: Keeping the customer informed throughout the repair process is critical for building trust and managing expectations. This includes providing regular updates on the status of the repair, any unexpected issues that arise, and the estimated time and cost of completion.
4. Use nonverbal communication: Nonverbal communication, such as facial expressions and body language, can also be important in conveying information and building rapport with customers.
5. Practice empathy: Showing empathy and understanding for the customer's situation can help build a positive relationship and increase customer satisfaction. This means taking the time to understand their concerns and showing a willingness to help.
6. Use technology effectively: Technology can be a powerful tool for communication, but it should be used thoughtfully and appropriately. This includes using email, text, and other digital channels to provide updates and information, but also ensuring that personal communication is not lost.
7. Seek feedback: Finally, seeking feedback from customers and colleagues can help identify areas for improvement and ensure that communication is effective and well received.

By practicing these strategies, vehicle service center employees can develop effective
communication skills that help build trust with customers, improve efficiency and drive
business success.

Techniques for resolving customer complaints.

Resolving customer complaints is an important part of providing exceptional customer
service in a vehicle service center. Here are some techniques that can help effectively resolve customer complaints:

1. Listen actively: The first step in resolving a customer complaint is to listen actively and understand their perspective. This means allowing the customer to express their concerns and asking clarifying questions to ensure that you fully understand the issue.
2. Apologize and take ownership: It's important to take responsibility for any mistakes or issues and to apologize sincerely to the customer. This can help diffuse their frustration and demonstrate a willingness to make things right.
3. Offer a solution: Once you understand the issue, offer a solution that addresses the customer's concerns. This may involve offering a repair or replacement, providing a refund, or offering a discount or other compensation.
4. Follow up: Following up with the customer after the complaint has been resolved can help ensure their satisfaction and build trust. This may involve checking in to ensure that the issue has been fully resolved or offering additional assistance or support as needed.
5. Learn from the experience: Finally, it's important to learn from the experience and identify any areas for improvement. This may involve analyzing the root cause of the complaint and implementing changes to prevent similar issues from occurring in the future.

By using these techniques, vehicle service center employees can effectively resolve customer complaints, build trust with customers, and improve the overall customer experience.

Vehicle Service center management best practices

Effective management is essential for the success of any vehicle service center. Here are some best practices that can help ensure effective management:

1. Establish clear processes and procedures: Clearly defined processes and procedures can help ensure that work is completed consistently and efficiently. This includes establishing standards for repairs, scheduling appointments, and managing inventory.
2. Hire and train skilled employees: Hiring skilled technicians and support staff is critical for ensuring that work is completed accurately and efficiently. Ongoing training and development can also help employees stay up-to-date on the latest technologies and best practices.
3. Use technology to streamline operations: Technology can help streamline operations and improve efficiency in a variety of ways, such as by automating appointment scheduling, managing inventory, and tracking customer information.
4. Monitor and measure performance: Regularly monitoring and measuring performance can help identify areas for improvement and ensure that the service center is meeting business goals. This may include tracking key performance metrics, such as customer satisfaction, repair completion times, and profitability.
5. Provide exceptional customer service: Providing

exceptional customer service is critical for building a loyal customer base and driving business success. This means focusing on the customer experience at every touchpoint, from scheduling appointments to completing repairs.

6. Foster a positive workplace culture: Creating a positive workplace culture can help improve employee engagement, retention, and overall performance. This may involve fostering open communication, providing opportunities for growth and development, and recognizing employee achievements.

By following these best practices, vehicle service center managers can improve efficiency, boost customer satisfaction, and drive business success.

Effective vehicle service center leadership and team management

Effective leadership and team management are essential for the success of any vehicle service center. Here are some strategies that can help:

1. Set clear goals and expectations: Clearly defining goals and expectations can help ensure that everyone on the team is aligned and working towards the same objectives.
2. Lead by example: Leading by example can help establish a positive work culture and build trust with employees. This means setting high standards for yourself and demonstrating the behaviors and attitudes that you expect from your team.
3. Communicate effectively: Effective communication is critical for building trust and ensuring that work is

completed accurately and efficiently. This includes actively listening to employees, providing regular feedback and coaching, and keeping the team informed of any changes or updates.

4. Empower employees: Empowering employees to take ownership of their work can help boost morale and improve performance. This means providing opportunities for growth and development, delegating responsibilities, and encouraging employees to share their ideas and perspectives.Build a cohesive team: Building a cohesive team can help improve collaboration and productivity. This may involve organizing team-building activities, providing opportunities for cross-training, and recognizing and rewarding team achievements.

5. Manage conflict effectively: Conflict is inevitable in any workplace, but effective conflict management can help prevent issues from escalating and ensure that everyone on the team feels heard and respected.

6. Lead with empathy and emotional intelligence: Effective leaders recognize that their employees are people first and that building strong relationships requires empathy and emotional intelligence. This means taking the time to understand your employees' perspectives and needs, and showing compassion and support when they face personal or professional challenges.

By following these strategies, vehicle service center leaders can build a high-performing team that is engaged, motivated, and committed to providing exceptional customer service.

Vehicle Service Center processes and procedures

Effective processes and procedures are critical for the smooth and efficient operation of a vehicle service center. Here are some key areas where processes and procedures can help:

1. Scheduling: Establishing a clear process for scheduling appointments can help ensure that work is completed on time and that customers are kept informed of any delays or changes.
2. Repair and maintenance: Clearly defining repair and maintenance procedures can help ensure that work is completed accurately and efficiently and that any potential issues are identified and addressed before they become more serious.
3. Quality control: Implementing a quality control process can help ensure that work meets established standards for quality and safety and that any issues are identified and resolved before the vehicle is returned to the customer.
4. Inventory management: Developing a process for managing inventory can help ensure that the service center has the necessary parts and supplies on hand to complete repairs and maintenance while minimizing waste and excess inventory.
5. Customer communication: Establishing clear procedures for communicating with customers can help ensure that they are informed of any updates or changes and that their questions and concerns are addressed in a timely and effective manner.
6. Billing and payments: Establishing a clear process for billing and payments can help ensure that customers are charged accurately and that payments are received on

time.

By implementing clear and effective processes and procedures in these key areas, vehicle service centers can improve efficiency, minimize errors, and deliver exceptional customer service.

Resource allocation and optimization

Effective resource allocation and optimization are critical for the success of any vehicle service center. Here are some strategies that can help:

1. Analyze demand: Analyzing demand for different services and identifying peak periods can help service centers allocate resources more effectively. This may involve tracking historical data on service volumes, monitoring customer trends, and using forecasting tools to anticipate future demand.
2. Optimize scheduling: Scheduling appointments in a way that optimizes the use of available resources can help minimize wait times and improve efficiency. This may involve using scheduling software to automate the process, setting up flexible scheduling options, and monitoring appointment volumes to ensure that capacity is not exceeded.
3. Manage inventory: Managing inventory effectively can help service centers optimize resource utilization and minimize waste. This may involve implementing an inventory management system that tracks inventory levels in real time, establishing minimum and maximum inventory levels, and regularly monitoring inventory

turnover.

4. Invest in training and development: Investing in employee training and development can help service centers optimize resource utilization by improving employee skills and productivity. This may involve providing ongoing training on new technologies and best practices, offering cross-training opportunities, and encouraging employees to share their knowledge and expertise.

5. Automate processes: Automating manual processes can help service centers optimize resource utilization by minimizing errors, reducing processing time, and freeing up employees to focus on more value-added activities. This may involve implementing software solutions for appointment scheduling, inventory management, and billing and payments.

By implementing these strategies, vehicle service centers can optimize their use of
resources, improve efficiency and deliver exceptional customer service.

Overview of vehicle service center technology and tools

Vehicle service centers rely on a range of technology and tools to provide efficient and
effective services. Here are some of the key tools and technologies commonly used in
vehicle service centers:

1. Diagnostic tools: These tools help technicians identify and diagnose problems with vehicles. They can include hand-

held scanners, computerized diagnostic tools, and software that helps technicians analyze vehicle data.

2. Lifts and hoists: These tools are used to lift vehicles off the ground so that technicians can inspect and repair them more easily. They can include hydraulic lifts, scissor lifts, and portable lifts.

3. Tire changers and balancers: These tools are used to remove and replace tires on vehicles, and ensure that they are balanced properly. They can include manual and automatic tire changers and computerized balancers.

4. Alignment machines: These machines help technicians adjust the suspension and steering components of vehicles to ensure that they are properly aligned. They can include computerized alignment machines and laser alignment systems.

5. Customer relationship management (CRM) software: This software is used to manage customer data, track appointments, and schedule services. It can also help service centers send reminders to customers about upcoming appointments and promote services.

6. Point of sale (POS) systems: These systems are used to manage billing and payments, track inventory, and generate reports. They can also be used to process credit card payments and manage customer loyalty programs.

7. Workforce management software: This software is used to manage employee schedules, track hours worked, and monitor productivity. It can also help service centers optimize scheduling to ensure that they have enough technicians available to meet demand.

By using these tools and technologies, vehicle service centers can provide faster, more accurate services and enhance the overall customer experience.

Common vehicle service center software and applications

Vehicle service centers typically use various software and applications to streamline their operations and enhance their efficiency. Here are some common types of software and applications used in vehicle service centers:

1. Customer Relationship Management (CRM) Software: CRM software is used to manage customer data, appointments, and communications. It may include features such as appointment scheduling, customer database management, service history tracking, and communication tools for sending reminders and notifications to customers.
2. Point of Sale (POS) Software: POS software is used for billing and payments, inventory management, and generating reports. It may include features such as invoicing, payment processing, inventory tracking, and reporting on sales and revenue.
3. Diagnostic Software: Diagnostic software is used by technicians to identify and diagnose vehicle problems. It may include features such as scanning and reading vehicle data, identifying fault codes, and providing recommendations for repairs.
4. Inventory Management Software: Inventory management software is used to track and manage the inventory of parts and supplies in the service center. It may include features such as inventory tracking, reordering, and stock-level monitoring.
5. Workforce Management Software: Workforce

management software is used to manage employee schedules, track hours worked, and monitor productivity. It may include features such as scheduling, time tracking, and reporting on labor costs.

6. Accounting Software: Accounting software is used to manage financial transactions and track expenses, revenues, and profits. It may include features such as bookkeeping, financial reporting, and tax management.
7. Marketing and Communications Tools: Service centers may use marketing and communications tools such as email marketing software, social media management tools, and customer review management platforms to communicate with customers, promote services, and manage online reputation.
8. Vehicle Maintenance Software: Vehicle maintenance software is used to track and manage the maintenance schedules of vehicles, including routine maintenance tasks such as oil changes, filter replacements, and tire rotations.

These are just a few examples of the software and applications commonly used in vehicle service centers. The specific software and applications used may vary depending on the size and complexity of the service center and its operations.

Best practices for using service center tools to increase efficiency and productivity

Here are some best practices for using service center tools to increase efficiency and productivity:

1. Provide Training and Education: Ensure that your staff is trained on how to effectively and efficiently use the tools and software in the service center. Provide regular training sessions, workshops, and resources to keep them updated on the latest features and functionalities.

2. Standardize Processes: Establish standard operating procedures (SOPs) for using the tools and software in the service center. This helps ensure consistency and efficiency in how the tools are used by all staff members. SOPs should include step-by-step instructions, guidelines, and best practices for tool usage.

3. Regular Maintenance and Updates: Keep your tools and software up-to-date with the latest versions, patches, and upgrades. Regularly perform maintenance tasks such as calibrations, cleanings, and inspections to ensure optimal performance and longevity of the tools.

4. Utilize Automation Features: Many service center tools and software come with automation features that can help streamline processes and save time. Take advantage of these features, such as automated appointment scheduling, inventory tracking, and customer notifications, to increase efficiency.

5. Customize Settings to Your Needs: Tailor the settings of your tools and software to your specific service center's needs. Customize features, preferences, and workflows to align with your processes and requirements, which can enhance efficiency and productivity.

6. Monitor and Analyze Performance: Utilize reporting and analytics features of your tools and software to monitor performance and identify areas for improvement. Analyze data such as service times, technician productivity, and customer feedback to identify

bottlenecks, areas of improvement, and opportunities for efficiency gains.

7. Foster Collaboration and Communication: Encourage collaboration and communication among your staff members when using service center tools and software. Foster a culture of teamwork, where staff members can share insights, tips, and feedback on how to effectively use the tools and software to increase efficiency and productivity.

8. Continuously Improve and Adapt: Continuously review and assess your service center's operations to identify areas for improvement. Stay updated with the latest advancements in tools and software and adapt your processes accordingly to leverage new features and functionalities.

By following these best practices, you can effectively use service center tools and software to increase efficiency and productivity, leading to improved customer service, reduced downtime, and increased profitability.

Overview of key performance metrics

Key performance metrics, also known as key performance indicators (KPIs), are measurable values used to evaluate the performance and effectiveness of a vehicle service center. These metrics provide insights into how well the service center is performing in various areas and can help identify areas for improvement. Here are some common key performance metrics used in vehicle service centers:

1. Customer Satisfaction: This metric measures the level of

satisfaction or happiness of customers with the service center's overall service quality, responsiveness, and communication. It can be assessed through customer surveys, feedback, online reviews, and ratings.

2. Service Turnaround Time: This metric measures the time it takes to complete a service or repair job, from the moment the vehicle enters the service center to the moment it is returned to the customer. It reflects the efficiency of the service center's processes and impacts the customer experience.

3. Service Technician Productivity: This metric measures the productivity and efficiency of service technicians, including the number of vehicles serviced, jobs completed, and labor hours worked. It provides insights into the performance of technicians and their ability to meet service demands.

4. First-time Fix Rate: This metric measures the percentage of vehicles that are fixed correctly on the first visit to the service center, without the need for rework or additional repairs. A higher first-time fix rate indicates a higher quality of repairs and reduces customer callbacks and rework costs.

5. Parts Fill Rate: This metric measures the percentage of times that required parts are available in the service center when needed for repairs. A higher parts fill rate indicates efficient parts management and reduces delays in repairs due to parts unavailability.

6. Repair Order (RO) Cycle Time: This metric measures the time it takes to complete a repair order, from the time it is opened to the time it is closed. It includes time spent on diagnosis, repairs, parts procurement, and administrative tasks. A shorter RO cycle time indicates

faster and more efficient service center operations.

7. Service Center Utilization: This metric measures the percentage of time that service bays or technicians are utilized for servicing vehicles. It reflects the efficiency and capacity utilization of the service center's resources.
8. Repeat Visits: This metric measures the percentage of customers who return to the service center for additional repairs or services within a specific timeframe. Higher repeat visit rates indicate customer loyalty and satisfaction, as well as opportunities for upselling or cross-selling.
9. Revenue and Profitability: These metrics measure the service center's financial performance, including revenue, gross profit margin, and net profit margin. They provide insights into the service center's financial health, efficiency in managing costs, and overall profitability.
10. Employee Morale and Retention: These metrics measure employee satisfaction, engagement, and retention rates within the service center. Higher employee morale and retention rates are indicative of a positive work environment and can contribute to improved performance and customer service.

These are just some examples of key performance metrics that can be used to assess the performance of a vehicle service center. The specific metrics used may vary depending on the goals, priorities, and operations of the service center, and it's important to select metrics that align with the overall objectives of the business. Regular monitoring and analysis of these key performance metrics can help identify areas for improvement, measure progress, and make data-driven decisions to enhance the performance and success of the vehicle service center.

Best practices for measuring and analyzing vehicle service center performance

Measuring and analyzing vehicle service center performance is crucial for identifying areas of improvement, optimizing operations, and ensuring customer satisfaction. Here are some best practices for effectively measuring and analyzing vehicle service center performance:

1. Define Clear Objectives: Clearly define the objectives and goals of the service center, and align them with the overall business goals. This will provide a framework for selecting appropriate performance metrics and measuring progress toward these objectives.
2. Select Relevant Metrics: Choose key performance metrics that are relevant to your service center's operations, goals, and customer expectations. Avoid overwhelming yourself with too many metrics and focus on those that are most meaningful to your specific service center.
3. Use Quantitative and Qualitative Data: Utilize both quantitative and qualitative data to gain a comprehensive understanding of service center performance. Quantitative data, such as metrics and numerical measurements, provide objective insights, while qualitative data, such as customer feedback and employee input, provide valuable subjective insights.
4. Establish Baselines and Targets: Establish baseline performance metrics to serve as a reference point for measuring progress. Set realistic targets or benchmarks

for each performance metric to strive for, based on industry standards, historical data, and business objectives.

5. Implement Reliable Data Collection and Reporting Systems: Ensure that your service center has reliable data collection and reporting systems in place to accurately capture and analyze performance data. Use software, tools, and technology solutions that automate data collection and reporting processes to minimize human errors and ensure consistency.

6. Regular Monitoring and Analysis: Continuously monitor and analyze performance
metrics regularly to track progress, identify trends, and uncover areas for improvement. Use data visualization techniques, such as charts and dashboards, to make performance data easily understandable and accessible.

7. Conduct Root Cause Analysis: When performance metrics fall short of targets or
expectations, conduct root cause analysis to identify the underlying causes of the issues. This may involve investigating process inefficiencies, resource constraints, training gaps, or other contributing factors that may impact performance.

8. Involve Employees: Involve employees at all levels in the measurement and analysis process. Encourage their participation in providing feedback, suggestions, and insights on service center performance. Employees on the front lines of service delivery can provide valuable information and ideas for improvement.

9. Take Action and Implement Improvements: Based on the insights gained from
performance measurement and analysis, take proactive

actions to implement
improvements in service center operations, processes,
and procedures. Continuously
monitor the impact of these improvements on
performance metrics and adjust as needed.
10. Communicate Findings and Results: Communicate the
findings and results of
performance measurement and analysis to all relevant
stakeholders, including
employees, management, and customers. This fosters
transparency, accountability, and a culture of continuous
improvement in the service center.

By following these best practices, you can effectively measure
and analyze vehicle service center performance, identify areas
for improvement, and implement strategies to optimize
operations and enhance customer satisfaction. Regular
performance measurement and analysis are essential for
maintaining a high level of service quality and achieving long-
term success in the competitive vehicle service industry.

***Developing performance improvement plans based on metrics
and analysis***

Developing performance improvement plans based on metrics
and analysis is a critical step in optimizing vehicle service center
operations and enhancing overall performance. Here are some
steps to develop effective performance improvement plans:

1. Review Performance Metrics: Review the performance
metrics that have been measured and analyzed for your
vehicle service center. Identify the areas where

performance falls short of targets or expectations and prioritize them based on their impact on overall service center performance.

2. Conduct Root Cause Analysis: Dig deeper into the underlying causes of performance issues by conducting a root cause analysis. Identify the underlying factors, such as process inefficiencies, resource constraints, skill gaps, or other contributing factors that are driving the performance gaps.
3. Set Specific and Measurable Goals: Set specific and measurable goals for each performance improvement area based on the findings from the root cause analysis.
4. Goals should be realistic, achievable, and aligned with the overall objectives of the service center.
5. Identify Improvement Strategies: Develop strategies and action plans to address the identified performance gaps. This may involve revising processes, improving resource allocation, providing training or coaching to employees, or implementing new technologies or tools to streamline operations.
6. Involve Employees: Involve employees at all levels in the development of performance improvement plans. Seek their input, feedback, and suggestions on strategies and actions to improve performance. Employees on the front lines of service delivery often have valuable insights and ideas for improvement.
7. Assign Responsibilities and Deadlines: Assign responsibilities for each improvement strategy or action plan, and set deadlines for completion. Ensure that there is clear ownership and accountability for the execution of the improvement

plans.

8. Monitor Progress: Regularly monitor the progress of the performance improvement plans to ensure that they are being implemented effectively. Track key performance metrics to measure the impact of the improvement plans and adjust strategies as needed.

9. Provide Support and Resources: Provide necessary support, resources, and training to employees to help them successfully implement the improvement plans. This may involve providing additional training, allocating resources, or addressing any obstacles or challenges that may arise during the implementation process.

10. Communicate Results: Communicate the results of the performance improvement efforts to all relevant stakeholders, including employees, management, and customers. Share the progress made, achievements, and impact on performance metrics. This fosters transparency, accountability, and a culture of continuous improvement in the service center.

11. Review and Adjust: Regularly review and adjust the performance improvement plans based on the feedback received from employees, the results achieved, and any changes in business objectives or external factors. Continuously strive to optimize operations and drive performance improvements.

By following these steps, you can develop effective performance improvement plans based on metrics and analysis, and systematically address performance gaps in your vehicle service center. Continuous improvement efforts based on data-driven insights are crucial for maintaining a high level of service quality, increasing customer satisfaction, and achieving long-term success in the competitive vehicle service industry.

Importance of employee engagement for service center performance

Employee engagement is a critical factor that directly impacts the performance of a vehicle service center. Engaged employees are those who are emotionally invested in their work, committed to their organization's goals, and motivated to go above and beyond their job requirements. When employees are engaged, they are more likely to be productive, provide exceptional customer service, and contribute positively to the overall performance of the service center. Here are some key reasons why employee engagement is important for service center performance:

1. Higher Productivity: Engaged employees tend to be more productive as they are
    motivated, committed, and enthusiastic about their work. They are willing to put in extra effort to achieve their goals and contribute to the success of the service center. This increased productivity can result in higher service center performance, faster turnaround times, and improved efficiency.

2. Improved Customer Service: Engaged employees are more likely to deliver exceptional customer service. They have a positive attitude towards customers, take ownership of their work, and are willing to go the extra mile to ensure customer satisfaction. Engaged employees build strong relationships with customers, leading to increased loyalty, repeat business, and positive word-of-

mouth recommendations.

3. Higher Retention and Lower Turnover: Engaged employees are more likely to be committed to their organization and less likely to leave. They are more satisfied with their work, feel valued, and have a sense of belonging. This can result in lower turnover rates, which in turn reduces recruitment and training costs associated with high employee turnover. It also helps in retaining experienced employees who possess valuable skills and knowledge that contribute to the overall performance of the service center.

4. Better Problem-Solving and Innovation: Engaged employees are more likely to actively participate in problem-solving and contribute innovative ideas to improve processes, systems, and customer service. They feel empowered and motivated to make a positive impact on the service center's performance. This can lead to continuous improvement initiatives, increased efficiency, and innovation in service delivery.

5. Positive Work Culture: Employee engagement fosters a positive work culture where employees feel valued, recognized, and appreciated. It creates a supportive and collaborative environment where employees are encouraged to communicate, collaborate, and share ideas. A positive work culture boosts morale, enhances teamwork, and promotes a sense of ownership and accountability, all of which contribute to improved service center performance.

6. Enhanced Employee Morale and Well-being: Engaged employees are more likely to have higher morale, job satisfaction, and overall well-being. They are less likely to

experience burnout or stress-related issues, leading to better physical and mental health. This results in higher attendance, fewer absences, and increased overall productivity.

In conclusion, employee engagement is a critical factor that directly impacts the performance of a vehicle service center. Engaged employees are more productive, provide exceptional customer service, contribute to a positive work culture, and actively participate in problem-solving and innovation. Investing in employee engagement initiatives can lead to improved service center performance, increased customer satisfaction, higher retention rates, and long-term success in the competitive service industry.

Strategies for improving employee engagement and motivation

Improving employee engagement and motivation is crucial for enhancing the overall
performance of a vehicle service center. Here are some strategies that can be implemented to improve employee engagement and motivation:

1. Clearly Communicate Expectations: Ensure that employees have a clear understanding of their roles, responsibilities, and performance expectations. Clearly communicate performance goals, targets, and deadlines, and provide regular feedback on their performance. This helps employees understand their importance in the service center and align their efforts toward achieving organizational goals.

2. Provide Opportunities for Growth and Development: Offer training programs, workshops, and professional development opportunities to help employees enhance their skills, knowledge, and career growth. This shows employees that the organization is invested in their growth and development and motivates them to perform better and advance in their careers.

3. Recognize and Reward Performance: Recognize and reward employees for their achievements, contributions, and efforts. This can be in the form of verbal appreciation, written notes, or tangible rewards such as incentives, bonuses, or promotions. Recognition and rewards make employees feel valued and appreciated and encourage them to continue their positive performance.

4. Foster a Positive Work Environment: Create a positive work culture that promotes open communication, teamwork, and collaboration. Encourage employees to share their ideas, opinions, and feedback. Provide a supportive and inclusive work environment where employees feel safe, respected, and heard. A positive work environment boosts employee morale, engagement, and motivation.

5. Empower Employees: Provide employees with the authority, autonomy, and resources to make decisions and take ownership of their work. Empower employees to contribute their ideas, insights, and suggestions. Involve them in decision-making processes, and give them opportunities to take on challenging tasks and projects. This instills a sense of ownership and accountability and motivates employees to perform at their best.

6. Foster Strong Leadership: Effective leadership plays a crucial role in employee engagement and motivation. Ensure that service center leaders are supportive, approachable, and lead by example. Provide leadership training and development opportunities to enhance their skills in managing and motivating employees. Strong leadership builds trust, respect, and loyalty among employees, which positively impacts their engagement and motivation.

7. Encourage Work-Life Balance: Recognize the importance of work-life balance and support employees in maintaining a healthy work-life balance. Avoid overloading employees with excessive workloads or unrealistic expectations, and encourage them to take breaks, vacations, and time off when needed. This helps employees manage their personal and professional commitments effectively, reducing stress and burnout, and increasing their motivation and engagement.

8. Foster Teamwork and Collaboration: Encourage teamwork, collaboration, and a positive team spirit among employees. Provide opportunities for team-building activities, cross-functional projects, and collaborative problem-solving. Teamwork fosters a sense of belonging, enhances employee engagement, and promotes a collaborative work environment.

9. Solicit and Act on Employee Feedback: Regularly seek feedback from employees through surveys, feedback sessions, and suggestion boxes. Act on the feedback received and implement changes based on the input provided by employees. This shows employees that their opinions are valued and encourages them to be more engaged and invested in their work.

10. Promote a Healthy Work-Life Balance: Recognize the importance of work-life balance and support employees in maintaining a healthy balance between their personal and professional lives. Avoid overloading employees with excessive workloads or unrealistic expectations, and encourage them to take breaks, vacations, and time off when needed. This helps employees manage their personal and professional commitments effectively, reducing stress and burnout, and increasing their motivation and engagement.

By implementing these strategies, a vehicle service center can create a supportive and engaging work environment that motivates employees to perform at their best, leading to improved engagement, productivity, and overall service center performance.

Best practices for employee training and development

Employee training and development are critical for enhancing the skills, knowledge, and
performance of employees in a vehicle service center. Here are some best practices for
effective employee training and development:

1. Identify Training Needs: Conduct a thorough analysis of the skills, knowledge, and performance gaps of employees to identify their training needs. This can be done through performance evaluations, feedback sessions, and discussions with employees and supervisors. Understanding the specific training needs of employees helps in designing targeted training programs that address those gaps.

2. Set Clear Training Objectives: Clearly define the objectives and outcomes of the training program. What do you want employees to learn or achieve through the training? Set specific, measurable, attainable, relevant, and time-bound (SMART) training objectives that align with the overall goals and objectives of the vehicle service center.

3. Use a Variety of Training Methods: Utilize a variety of training methods to cater to different learning styles and preferences of employees. This can include on-the-job training, classroom training, e-learning, workshops, simulations, role-plays, and other interactive learning methods. Mix and match training methods to create a well-rounded training program.

4. Provide Relevant and Timely Training: Ensure that the training provided is relevant to the job responsibilities and tasks of the employees. The training content should be up-to-date and aligned with the latest industry standards and best practices. Deliver the training promptly, so that employees can apply the knowledge and skills gained in their day-to-day work.

5. Engage and Involve Employees: Actively involve employees in the training process to enhance their engagement and participation. Encourage them to ask

questions, share their experiences, and provide feedback. Provide opportunities for hands-on learning, problem-solving, and practical application of the training concepts. Engaged employees are more likely to retain and apply the training in their work.

6. Provide Ongoing Training and Development: Training and development should not be a one-time event, but an ongoing process. Continuously provide opportunities for employees to enhance their skills, knowledge, and capabilities. Offer refresher courses, advanced training, and professional development programs to help employees stay updated and grow in their roles.

7. Support Continuous Learning: Foster a culture of continuous learning in the vehicle service center. Encourage employees to seek out learning opportunities, share knowledge with their peers, and stay updated with industry trends and advancements. Provide access to resources such as books, articles, online courses, and industrypublications to support their continuous learning journey.

8. Evaluate Training Effectiveness: Regularly evaluate the effectiveness of the training programs to ensure that they are meeting the intended objectives. Use feedback from employees, supervisors, and other stakeholders to assess the impact of the training on their performance. Identify areas for improvement and make necessary adjustments to the training programs to enhance their effectiveness.

9. Recognize and Reward Learning and Development: Recognize and reward employees who actively participate in training and development programs and apply the acquired knowledge and skills in their work. This can be in the form of verbal appreciation,

certificates, promotions, or other tangible rewards. Recognizing and rewarding learning and development efforts motivate employees to engage in further training and development activities.

10. Provide Supportive Follow-up: Provide post-training support to employees to reinforce the learning and ensure its application in the workplace. This can include coaching, mentoring, and providing opportunities for the practical application of the training concepts.

Follow-up support helps employees overcome challenges and reinforces the training,
leading to better retention and application of the learned skills. By following these best practices, a vehicle service center can create an effective employee training and development program that enhances the skills, knowledge, and performance of
employees, leading to improved service center performance and customer satisfaction.

The importance of continuous improvement in vehicle service center performance

Continuous improvement is crucial for vehicle service center performance as it helps to
drive ongoing progress, optimize operations, and enhance customer satisfaction. Here are some key reasons why continuous improvement is essential in the context of vehicle service center performance:

1. Enhanced Efficiency and Productivity: Continuous

improvement efforts focus on

2. identifying and eliminating inefficiencies, bottlenecks, and waste in service center processes. By continuously evaluating and refining operations, service centers can streamline workflows, reduce cycle times, and improve resource utilization, leading to increased efficiency and productivity.

3. Improved Quality and Customer Satisfaction: Continuous improvement involves
identifying and addressing the root causes of service failures, defects, and customer
complaints. By systematically analyzing and improving service center processes, service centers can enhance the quality of services delivered to customers, resulting in higher customer satisfaction and loyalty.

4. Cost Reduction and Resource Optimization: Continuous improvement efforts help in identifying and eliminating non-value-added activities, unnecessary costs, and resource wastage. By optimizing resource allocation and utilization, service centers can reduce operational costs, maximize returns on investment, and improve profitability.

5. Innovation and Adaptability: Continuous improvement encourages a culture of
innovation, experimentation, and learning in the service center. It fosters a mindset of constantly seeking better ways of doing things, challenging the status quo, and adapting to changing customer needs, market trends, and technological advancements.

6. Employee Engagement and Development: Continuous improvement involves engaging employees in identifying improvement opportunities, implementing changes, and

monitoring results. It empowers employees to take ownership of their work and contribute to the success of the service center. This leads to increased employee engagement, motivation, and development.

7. Competitive Advantage: In today's competitive business environment, service centers need to constantly strive for improvement to stay ahead of the competition. Continuous improvement efforts can help service centers differentiate themselves by delivering superior services, faster response times, and higher customer satisfaction levels, leading to a competitive advantage in the market.

8. Compliance and Risk Management: Continuous improvement also includes monitoring and managing compliance with industry regulations, safety standards, and legal requirements. By continuously evaluating and improving compliance processes, service centers can mitigate risks, avoid penalties, and safeguard their reputation.

In summary, continuous improvement is vital for vehicle service center performance as it enables service centers to optimize operations, enhance customer satisfaction, reduce costs, foster innovation, engage employees, gain a competitive edge, and ensure compliance with regulations. It is an ongoing process that requires a proactive mindset, a culture of continuous learning, and a commitment to excellence.

Identifying and prioritizing areas for improvement

Identifying and prioritizing areas for improvement is a critical step in the continuous improvement process for vehicle service centers. Here are some best practices for identifying and prioritizing areas for improvement:

1. Data-driven Analysis: Utilize data and metrics to identify areas where performance is subpar or below expectations. This can include analyzing key performance indicators (KPIs) such as customer satisfaction scores, service time, service revenue, repeat customer rate, employee productivity, and other relevant metrics. Data-driven analysis provides an objective and factual basis for identifying areas that require improvement.
2. Customer Feedback: Solicit feedback from customers through surveys, reviews, and complaints to identify pain points, areas of dissatisfaction, and opportunities for improvement. Customers' feedback is invaluable in identifying areas that directly impact their experience and satisfaction with the service center.
3. Employee Input: Involve employees at all levels in the identification process, as they are often on the front lines and have insights into operational challenges and improvement opportunities. Encourage employees to provide feedback and suggestions for improvement based on their day-to-day experiences and interactions with customers and processes.
4. Process Mapping and Analysis: Conduct process mapping exercises to visually map out current processes and identify bottlenecks, redundancies, and areas of inefficiency. This can help uncover areas that need improvement in terms of process flow, resource allocation, and task sequencing.
5. Root Cause Analysis: Use root cause analysis techniques, such as the 5 Whys, Fishbone Diagrams, or Pareto Analysis, to identify the underlying causes of problems or

performance gaps. This helps to identify the true root causes rather than addressing symptoms, enabling targeted improvement efforts.

6. Prioritization Matrix: Use a prioritization matrix or other decision-making tools to prioritize improvement areas based on factors such as impact, feasibility, and urgency. This helps to objectively prioritize improvement areas and allocate resources accordingly.

7. Alignment with Business Goals: Ensure that the identified improvement areas align with the overall business goals and objectives of the vehicle service center. This ensures that improvement efforts are aligned with the strategic direction of the organization and contribute to its overall success.

Once areas for improvement are identified, it is important to prioritize them based on their impact, feasibility, and urgency. This allows the service center to focus its efforts and resources on areas that will yield the greatest improvement in performance. Regular review and monitoring of progress against improvement initiatives should be conducted to ensure that the desired outcomes are achieved and sustained over time.

Implementing continuous improvement initiatives and measuring their impact

Implementing continuous improvement initiatives in a vehicle service center is an ongoing process that involves several key steps. Here are some best practices for implementing and measuring the impact of continuous improvement initiatives:

1. Plan and Set Clear Objectives: Develop a clear plan

that outlines the specific objectives, goals, and timelines for each improvement initiative. Ensure that the objectives are measurable, realistic, and aligned with the overall business goals of the service center.

2. Assign Responsibility and Accountability: Assign clear responsibility and accountability for each improvement initiative to specific team members or departments. Clearly communicate their roles and responsibilities, and empower them with the authority and resources needed to implement the initiatives effectively.

3. Implement Changes and Monitor Progress: Implement the identified improvement initiatives and closely monitor their progress. Regularly review and analyze data and metrics to assess the effectiveness of the initiatives in achieving the desired outcomes. This may include tracking KPIs, customer feedback, employee feedback, and other relevant metrics.

4. Review and Adjust as Needed: Conduct periodic reviews of the improvement initiatives to assess their impact and identify any adjustments or modifications that may be needed. This may involve conducting a root cause analysis of any unexpected outcomes or gaps and making necessary adjustments to the initiatives or implementation approach.

5. Employee Involvement and Communication: Involve employees at all levels in the implementation of improvement initiatives. Engage them in the process, provide regular updates on progress, and encourage their feedback and suggestions for further improvement. Effective communication and employee involvement are crucial for the success of continuous

improvement initiatives.

6. Training and Development: Provide necessary training and development opportunities to employees to equip them with the skills and knowledge needed to implement and sustain the improvement initiatives. This may include providing training on new processes, technologies, tools, or skills that are required for the successful implementation of the initiatives.

7. Celebrate Successes and Recognize Efforts: Acknowledge and celebrate the successes and achievements resulting from the continuous improvement initiatives. Recognize and reward the efforts of employees who have contributed to the success of the initiatives. This promotes a positive culture of continuous improvement and motivates employees to continue their efforts toward improving performance.

8. Review and Share Best Practices: Regularly review and share best practices within the service center and with other relevant stakeholders. This includes documenting and sharing lessons learned, successes, and challenges encountered during the implementation of the improvement initiatives.

This helps to institutionalize the culture of continuous improvement and facilitates knowledge sharing across the organization. Measuring the impact of continuous improvement initiatives can be done through regular monitoring and analysis of data and metrics. This may include tracking key performance indicators (KPIs) before and after the implementation of the initiatives, conducting customer surveys and feedback analysis, analyzing employee feedback and engagement levels, and conducting regular reviews and assessments of the overall performance of the service center. The data and insights obtained from these measurements can help in evaluating the effectiveness of the improvement initiatives and making informed decisions on further improvements or adjustments as needed.

Summary of key takeaways and Strategies for improving service center performance

Summary of Key Takeaways:

1. Vehicle service center performance is critical for customer satisfaction and business success, and it can be measured using various key performance metrics such as customer satisfaction, service quality, employee productivity, and financial performance.
2. Developing exceptional customer service involves understanding customer needs and expectations, effective communication skills, prompt resolution of customer complaints, and exceeding customer expectations through personalized and professional service.
3. Vehicle service center performance can be improved through effective leadership and team management, streamlined processes and procedures, optimized resource allocation, and leveraging technology and tools to increase efficiency and productivity.
4. Continuous improvement is essential for service center performance, and it involves planning, implementing, monitoring, reviewing, and adjusting improvement initiatives based on data and metrics, involving

employees at all levels, providing training and development opportunities, and celebrating successes and recognizing efforts.

Strategies for Improving Service Center Performance:

1. Prioritize customer satisfaction: Understand and meet customer needs and expectations through personalized and professional service, prompt resolution of complaints, and exceeding customer expectations.
2. Streamline processes and procedures: Regularly review and optimize service center processes and procedures to eliminate bottlenecks, reduce waste, and improve overall efficiency and productivity.
3. Optimize resource allocation: Efficiently allocate resources such as manpower, equipment, and inventory to ensure optimal utilization and minimize unnecessary costs.
4. Leverage technology and tools: Utilize appropriate software applications and tools to automate processes, track performance metrics, and streamline operations for improved efficiency and effectiveness.
5. Develop effective leadership and team management: Provide strong leadership and effective team management, including clear communication, regular feedback, and recognition of employee efforts, to foster a positive and motivated work environment.
6. Invest in employee training and development: Provide ongoing training and development opportunities for employees to enhance their skills, knowledge, and capabilities, and empower them to contribute to service

center performance
improvement initiatives.

7. Foster a culture of continuous improvement: Encourage
   and involve employees at all levels in the identification,
   implementation, and measurement of improvement
   initiatives, and promote a culture of continuous learning
   and improvement.

8. Monitor and measure performance: Regularly monitor
   and measure performance using key performance
   metrics, analyze data, and use insights to identify areas
   for improvement, make informed decisions, and adjust
   strategies as needed.

9. Foster positive customer and employee relationships:
   Cultivate positive relationships with customers and
   employees through effective communication, prompt
   resolution of complaints, and recognition of employee
   efforts, as this can contribute to improved service center
   performance.

10. Continuously review and adjust strategies: Continuously
    review and adjust strategies based on data, feedback,
    and performance metrics, and adapt to changing business
    needs and market conditions for sustained service center
    performance improvement.

By implementing these strategies and continuously monitoring
and measuring
performance, vehicle service centers can optimize their
operations, enhance customer
satisfaction, and achieve business success.

***Developing an action plan for implementing performance
improvement initiatives***

Developing an action plan for implementing performance improvement initiatives involves several key steps. Here's an overview of the process:

1. Identify performance improvement opportunities: Conduct a thorough review of the current performance metrics, processes, and procedures of the vehicle service center to identify areas that require improvement. This can be done through data analysis, customer feedback, employee input, and benchmarking against industry best practices.
2. Set clear and measurable goals: Define specific, measurable, achievable, relevant, and time-bound (SMART) goals that align with the overall objectives of the service center. These goals should be realistic and achievable, considering the available resources and constraints.
3. Develop improvement strategies: Based on the identified performance improvement opportunities, develop strategies and action plans to address each area for improvement. These strategies should be specific, actionable, and aligned with the overall goals and objectives of the service center.
4. Assign responsibilities and establish timelines: Clearly define roles and responsibilities for each improvement initiative and establish timelines for completion. Assign accountability to relevant team members to ensure ownership and accountability for the success of the initiatives.
5. Allocate resources: Identify the resources required for implementing the improvement initiatives, including

manpower, equipment, technology, and budget. Allocate resources effectively to ensure the smooth execution of the action plans.

6. Communicate and engage employees: Communicate the performance improvement initiatives and their objectives to all relevant employees. Foster employee engagement by involving them in the process, seeking their input, and providing training and support as needed.

7. Monitor and measure progress: Establish monitoring mechanisms to track the progress of each improvement initiative against the set goals and timelines. Regularly review and analyze data and metrics to measure the impact of the initiatives and identify any deviations or areas that require adjustment.

8. Review and adjust the action plan: Based on the progress and results, conduct periodic reviews of the action plan and adjust strategies as needed. Make informed decisions to reallocate resources, revise timelines, or modify strategies to ensure continuous improvement.

9. Celebrate successes and recognize efforts: Celebrate successes and recognize the efforts and achievements of employees involved in the performance improvement initiatives. This can boost employee morale, motivation, and commitment to further improvement efforts.

10. Continuously improve: Performance improvement is an ongoing process, and it's
important to continuously review, analyze, and improve performance to sustain progress and achieve long-term success.

By following these steps and regularly reviewing and adjusting the action plan based on

progress and results, a vehicle service center can effectively implement performance
improvement initiatives and achieve sustained improvements in key performance areas.

Best in class and competitive edge.

All these efforts aim to Give your Business a competitive edge. These are the qualities that offer unique and distinct advantages over competitors. These areas typically include the following

1. Unique Value Proposition: A compelling value proposition that sets the business apart from competitors by offering unique and superior products, services, or solutions to customers. This could be through innovative features, superior quality, competitive pricing, exceptional customer service, or other differentiating factors.
2. Brand Reputation: A positive and well-established brand reputation that creates customer trust, loyalty, and recognition. A strong brand reputation can give a business a competitive advantage by influencing customer purchasing decisions and attracting new customers.
3. Customer Relationships: Strong and loyal customer relationships built on trust, excellent customer service, and personalized experiences. This includes understanding and fulfilling customer needs, providing exceptional after-sales support, and maintaining open lines of communication to build long-term relationships and customer loyalty.
4. Market Positioning: A strategic positioning in the market

that differentiates the business from competitors. This includes understanding the target market, identifying gaps or unmet needs, and positioning the business as the preferred choice in the minds of customers.

5. Innovation and Technology: Continuous innovation and adoption of new technologies to stay ahead of competitors and provide unique products, services, or processes that deliver superior performance, efficiency, or convenience. This can include investment in research and development, staying up-to-date with industry trends, and leveraging advanced technologies to gain a competitive edge.

6. Operational Efficiency: Efficient and effective operational processes that enable the business to deliver products or services in a cost-effective and timely manner. This includes streamlined workflows, optimized supply chains, effective inventory management, and other operational strategies that minimize costs, reduce waste, and enhance productivity.

7. Human Capital: A highly skilled and motivated workforce that contributes to the business's competitive advantage. This includes attracting and retaining top talent, providing ongoing training and development opportunities, fostering a positive work culture, and empowering employees to contribute their best to the business.

8. Customer Insights and Data Analytics: Utilizing customer insights and data analytics to make informed business decisions, identify new opportunities, and optimize strategies. This includes analyzing customer data, market research, and industry trends to gain valuable insights that can inform strategic decisions and give the business

a competitive edge.

9. Customer Experience: Delivering exceptional customer experiences at every touchpoint, from initial contact to after-sales support. This includes providing personalized and convenient experiences, resolving customer issues promptly and effectively, and continually improving the overall customer journey to exceed customer expectations.

10. Flexibility and Agility: The ability to adapt and respond quickly to changing market conditions, customer needs, and competitive pressures. This includes the ability to pivot strategies, make informed decisions in a dynamic business environment, and seize opportunities to stay ahead of competitors.

Overall, a competitive edge is achieved by leveraging unique and distinct advantages that set a business apart from competitors, create value for customers, and enable the business to outperform the competition in the market. Making your business among the best in class in your market.